Hand Lettering God's Love

Drawing God's Word into Your Heart through the Craft of Brush Lettering

Margaret Feinberg
and Jessica Taylor Design

BETHANY HOUSE PUBLISHERS
a division of Baker Publishing Group
Minneapolis, Minnesota

Abide in my love
John 15:9 NASB

© 2017 by Margaret Feinberg, LLC (www.margaretfeinberg.com)

Published by Bethany House Publishers
11400 Hampshire Avenue South
Bloomington, Minnesota 55438
www.bethanyhouse.com

Bethany House Publishers is a division of
Baker Publishing Group, Grand Rapids, Michigan

Printed in the United States of America

ISBN 978-0-7642-3178-0

Scripture quotations marked HCSB are from the Holman Christian Standard Bible, copyright 1999, 2000, 2002, 2003 by Holman Bible Publishers. Used by permission.

Scripture quotations marked MSG are from *The Message* by Eugene H. Peterson, copyright © 1993, 1994, 1995, 2000, 2001, 2002. Used by permission of NavPress Publishing Group. All rights reserved.

Scripture quotations marked NASB are from the New American Standard Bible®, copyright © 1960, 1962, 1963, 1968, 1971, 1972, 1973, 1975, 1977, 1995 by The Lockman Foundation. Used by permission.

Scripture quotations marked NCV are from the New Century Version®. Copyright © 1987, 1988, 1991 by Word Publishing, a division of Thomas Nelson, Inc. Used by permission. All rights reserved.

Scripture quotations marked NIV are from the Holy Bible, New International Version®. NIV®. Copyright © 1973, 1978, 1984, 2011 by Biblica, Inc.™ Used by permission of Zondervan. All rights reserved worldwide. www.zondervan.com

Scripture quotations marked NKJV are from the New King James Version. Copyright © 1982 by Thomas Nelson, Inc. Used by permission. All rights reserved.

Scripture quotations marked NLT are from the *Holy Bible*, New Living Translation, copyright © 1996, 2004, 2007 by Tyndale House Foundation. Used by permission of Tyndale House Publishers, Inc., Carol Stream, Illinois 60188. All rights reserved.

Cover photo by Meghan Shaw Photography
Author photos by Audrey Hannah Photography and Rebecca Slaughter

17 18 19 20 21 22 23   7 6 5 4 3 2 1

Table of Contents

Your love is better than life.

psalm 63:3

Hello Beautiful

My mom returned home with a gift that stirred my childhood imagination—a pack of pens designed for drawing letters. I still remember those five colors—red, blue, green, brown, and black. I formed words and flourishes until the ink ran dry. Sculpting letters on a page provided space to doodle, design, and dream.

Sometimes I wonder if playing with all those letters inspired me to become a writer.

More recently, my heart awakened to new beauty with hand lettering appearing everywhere.

But I never thought I could create my own hand lettered images. *That's for the real artists, those with real talent, those with gobs of real time*, I told myself.

My sweet friend Jessica encouraged me, "You can do this! I'll help you."

Now I've worked with Jessica for the last decade as she managed my creative whirl-wind with clarity and gusto. As a successful womanpreneur, she launched Jessica Taylor Design. Her stunning hand lettering artwork, including, "Not Today, Satan," "Girl Boss," and "I'd walk across Legos for you" hang throughout our home.

I never dreamed I could make art like hers to enjoy or give to others.

Yet Jessica made it easy for me to learn. She told me the exact supplies to order online. Then she taught me letter by letter how to use a brush-pen.

I discovered that with the right coaching and practice, anyone can learn to hand letter.

This simple artistic expression reminded me of the importance of words—especially God's words. Fusing hand lettering with Scripture opened a new pathway to read and reflect on the Bible.

I can't keep this gift to myself. I want to share Jessica's amazing teaching and training with you. That's why we've created *Hand Lettering God's Love*.

We believe creativity is a gift of God—since God's the ultimate Creator. With every brush-stroke from the beginning of time, God has been writing a love letter to us and through us.

That's why we're inviting you to learn hand lettering and rediscover how you're created to experience and extend the love of God. After all, this is who you are and this is who you are called to be.

Together, let's uncap our creativity and grow closer to Jesus.

xoxo,
Margaret

Your Creative Gift

"But I'm not creative."

I've heard that same line from dozens of friends and relatives, neighbors and co-workers. Those syllables have even slipped out from my lips. Let's be honest: We may recognize something as beautiful, but creativity is for *that* type of person, *that* type of talent, *that* special gifting. Creativity has become a buzzword of exclusion and a breeding ground for inadequacy. "Creatives" are those with unkempt hair, paint smears on their arms, and mismatched socks.

Yet creativity is so much more.

Somewhere along the way, we lose the giddiness of the five-year-old galloping to show off their stick-figure doodles. We discover the shame and fear so closely associated with creativity. We soon miss the joy and delight that comes when we create something beautiful.

You may not consider yourself creative, but creativity is woven into your DNA, breathed into your bones. Maybe your creative muscles have atrophied in adulthood, but they are waiting to be softened. Maybe through dance, song, writing, painting, drawing, day-dreaming. Or maybe through decorating a room, planning a party, organizing a spreadsheet, cooking a savory meal, managing a staff, or arranging a calendar (especially with all those carpool-lane pickups and early morning swim meets).

You are created to create.

We are handcrafted by the Master Artist and invited to participate in this creative process.

Brush lettering is a way I've stretched my creative muscles, and I want you to come along. Whether you've never picked up a brush-pen in your life, or you're a total pro, this book will help you hone the artistic craft and draw you closer to God along the way.

Throughout this lettering journey, I've discovered a few gems.

Brush lettering reminds us that creativity takes courage.

A blank page can be intimidating. You don't know where or how to start. Courage isn't the act of getting rid of fear, but staring fear in the face and starting anyway.

Brush lettering challenges us to value community over competition.

We are reminded often that someone is better than us. A better parent. A better employee. A better friend. A better wife. Better time managers. But when we start seeing those around us as people to cheer on instead of compete with, we dislodge a creative block.

~ Brush lettering asks us to notice our progress over perfection.

Instead of saying: "Look how far you've come!" our inner critic often whispers: "Look how far you have to go." As a recovering perfectionist, I can nitpick every stray line, every misplaced letter, until I want to quit.

It's easy to tell ourselves we don't like something or it's tough or weird or uncomfortable and too soon give up. If you stick it out, you'll notice your progress. Take a risk on messy. As one of my favorite artists once said, "We don't make mistakes, just happy little accidents." *Thanks, Bob Ross.*

~ Brush lettering offers us the freedom to be fully ourselves.

We are tempted to don masks; we try to look and act like someone else. But each of us has a unique wiring and gifting, perspective and presence. The world is a better and more beautiful place because of the variety we bring to it. Brush lettering offers permission for you to be fully yourself.

We all begin with the same mediums—pens and blank sheets of paper—but what we produce will look wildly different because we see the world and recognize beauty through different lenses.

~ Brush lettering invites us to slow down and study Scripture.

Because of the leisurely pace of brush lettering, we're able to slow down and focus on every letter we create. That's why we've included Scripture as the basis for your practice throughout this book. We embed God's Word in our hearts as we form each verse.

What do you say? Will you wear your crown of creativity and dive into this practice with us?

Sometimes creativity flows from our fingertips and other times we'll have to force it, but even in the discipline, we rediscover the gifts of joining the Master Artist: rest, beauty, courage, and delight.

My hope is that you will hush the inner critic as we practice the creative discipline of brush lettering. And along the way, you'll rediscover the heights and depths, lengths and widths of God's love.

Let's get started.

Jess

P.S. We'd love to see and celebrate what you learn along the way. Snap photos to share on social media. Use #handletteringgodslove and tag us: @mafeinberg and @jessicataylordesign.

"Creativity is the way I share my soul with the world."
—Brené Brown

We Love Lefties

Jessica's sweet momma is a lefty, and we've heard her vent that the world was simply not made for her. She must search for a different pair of scissors, a different can opener, a different set of golf clubs, and re-seat herself at dinner parties to avoid dueling elbows. *Can you relate?*

We have good news. Mastering brush lettering is not out of reach for you. We'll be honest, some letters will be trickier. But the letters, shapes, and directions that are squirrelly for righties will be a breeze to your southpaw.

Here are tried and tested tips (thanks, Mom!) for our lovely lefty letterers.

The three main hand placements for lefties are:

1. **The hovering hand:** when your forearm rests on the paper, but your wrist and fingers float in the air. This technique can be tricky to control with brush-pens.
2. **The over hook:** when you curl your hand above the line you're writing on, often used by people who were taught to write by right-handers. This technique risks smudging.
3. **The under writer:** when the meat of the hand touches the paper for stability, but you stretch your fingers to write under the line of text. This will be the best hand placement for lettering; however, do what feels most natural to you.

Embrace the grace: Lefties will always wrestle with smudging. It's the nature of writing from left to right with your left hand. This is normal. Give yourself extra time in between shapes or letters so the ink has a chance to dry before you drag your hand over that area.

Transitions are difficult techniques for lefties to master. Because you're pushing down and pushing across toward the right (unlike righties who pull the pen down and pull across), it's an unnatural pressure and direction for the pen. For this reason, we recommend spending more time with the less-expensive pens (like Crayola Super Tips) before you switch to the more expensive pens (like Tombow Dual Brush Pens) so you don't fray them.

The key to mastering this transition is to start easing up on the pressure before you make the turn. Give yourself more time to transition the change in pressure. Taper the thick or add pressure to the thin before the turn.

Above all? Give yourself grace. Like any new skill, this one takes extra patience and practice.

Cheering you on,

Jess and Margaret

Before We Begin

Brush lettering is a skill that involves developing muscle memory. Also known as: Practice. Practice. Practice. You must master the basic strokes and skills so that advancing will come more naturally. From basic line drills to connecting letters, the skills build on each other. While it may be tempting, don't skip ahead. Love yourself enough to be patient.

Brush lettering is trickier than using a regular pen. Why? The flexible tip allows for a change in pressure. This art form offers you endless options when it comes to color, layout, and design. As you master the basics (as taught in this book), your own style will emerge on the paper. Many letters will evolve and continue evolving as you discover what feels most true to you.

Brush lettering is different for the left-handed. We're right-handed, but we know for our lovely lefty friends, learning to letter can take some extra work. Read through We Love Lefties on page 8 before continuing.

Through brush lettering, I'm reminded of the steady pace it takes to follow God, one foot in front of the other, one day at a time. It isn't easy right away, but after practice and persistence, I'm more able to extend grace, to offer forgiveness, to lavish people with love.

Brush lettering requires you to take your time. Move s.l.o.w.l.y. The slower you go, the more precise your work will be. We want you to feel successful at brush lettering. Don't feel rushed to move forward until you've mastered a step. Slow, consistent, and persistent are the key words when it comes to mastering brush lettering and growing in your faith.

Brush lettering differs from handwriting. Handwriting is quick and dirty. Brush lettering is slow and steady. Each letter is handcrafted and drawn with precision, as opposed to handwriting that can be inconsistent and difficult to read.

Brush lettering: *you are lovely*

My actual handwriting:
(please excuse the
chicken scratch) *You are lovely*

Brush lettering asks you to be gentle with yourself. This may not come naturally at first. Give yourself grace. You're doing something new, and we're so proud of you.

Your Toolbox

Here are our favorite must-haves when it comes to brush lettering. Don't worry, this doesn't have to empty your piggy bank. Don't get everything on the list. Just one pen and one type of paper will suffice. It's always helpful to have a pencil with a good eraser nearby.

If you're just getting started:

Crayola Super Tip Markers. These are inexpensive washable markers and come in a bouquet of colors. (You may already have some stashed in your kid's art supplies). While you won't get the flexibility of a higher quality brush-pen, these are awesome for practicing and just getting started. You'll find a pack of 10 on Amazon or at Target and WalMart for $5–$7.

If you're feeling a tad more confident:

Tombow Fudenosuke. These pens are used for writing kanji (Chinese characters). Often available on Amazon or a local art supply store for $7–$9, this is a pack of two pens: a soft, flexible tip and a more rigid tip. Begin with the more rigid tip (indicated in silver) for better control. Once you have that pen mastered, move to the more flexible tip (indicated in gold).

If you're ready to be a pro:

Tombow Dual Brush Pens. These markers are at the pricier end (a pack of 10 is around $26) and come in lots of colors. They include a bullet-tip side and a flexible tip. These nibs fray very easily if not used properly or on wrong paper. Hold off on investing in these until you're a more comfortable letterer.

Selecting your paper:

While you may be tempted to use any paper within reach, the fibers in textured papers will fray your brush pens and shorten their lifespan. Steer clear from sketchbooks, calligraphy paper, or watercolor paper to preserve the life of your precious pens. We recommend using extra smooth paper to protect your pens and markers like:

- **Printer paper that is specifically labeled as "smooth."** Pick up a ream of smooth printer paper from your local office supply store for $8–$12.

- **A Rhodia notebook or pad.** These come in many different sizes and designs (dot, grid, or blank)—choose which you love best. This notebook is also a great way to keep all of your practice in one place. You can find these on Amazon or in a local art supply store for $7–$12.

Simply visit margaretfeinberg.com/handlettering for links to all these products plus some fun training videos.

Bonus tip: Use tracing paper over the guides in this book so you can practice many times over. You can pick up a pack on Amazon or in a local art supply store for $5–$7.

Set Up for Success

How to arrange your paper:

If you're RIGHT-HANDED:

1. The LEFT edge of your paper should be in line with the center of your body.
2. Tilt the paper so the RIGHT top corner is higher than the LEFT side. The bottom LEFT corner should be closest to your body.

If you're LEFT-HANDED:

1. The RIGHT edge of your paper should be in line with the center of your body.
2. Tilt the paper so the LEFT top corner is higher than the RIGHT side. The bottom RIGHT corner should be closest to your body.

Well done!

How to hold your pen:

Have you noticed that everyone holds their pencils radically different? Some use two fingers, others one, others have a death grab (like Margaret). Do what feels comfortable to you. Don't make any changes to how you would normally hold a pencil.

Bonus tip: My most creative work is done in a life-giving space: a clutter-free table, comfy chair, and cozy blanket. I make sure to have a steaming cup of coffee nearby and music playing in the background. How can you make your creative space a place that brings you life?

This would be like learning to write with your opposite hand. Yikes! There's no need to retrain your brain to grip a pen differently.

You simply need to make three adjustments:

1. Scoot your grip up the pen so there's about an inch to an inch-and-a-half from your fingers to the paper. This will allow room for you to tilt the pen and make the transition from thick to thin (don't worry, I'll soon explain what that means).
2. Change the angle you hold a brush-pen. While writing with a normal pen or pencil, you will often hold your pen at a 90-degree angle, perpendicular to the paper. But brush lettering requires pens to be held at a 45-degree angle. This will give you flexibility to add and release pressure to the tip of the brush. If you attempt to hold a brush-pen at 90 degrees, you'll fray your pen by smooshing the tip into the paper.
3. Allow yourself extra elbow room. Brush lettering involves using your entire forearm to move the pen—not just the fingers or just the wrist.

Those are the basics.

The Anatomy of Letters

Cap height >
Ascender >
< Upstroke
Downstroke >
X-height >
Overshoot >
Baseline >
Descender >
Beard line >

My beloved

Here's the basic structure of brush lettering:

Ascender: The part of a letter that is taller than the x-height (like b or l). Often these extend above cap height.

Cap height: The height of a capital letter above the baseline.

X-height: The distance between the baseline and the height of lowercase letters. This is measured by the height of the lowercase letter x in the font (hence the name).

Overshoot: The distance a rounded lowercase letter (like e or o) exceeds the x-height.

Baseline: The line upon which most letters sit and below which descenders extend.

Descender: The part of a letter that extends below the baseline (like j or y).

Beard line: This is where descenders sit.

Upstroke: The thin, light-pressure stroke each time you move up with your pen.

Downstroke: The thick, heavy-pressure stroke each time you move down with your pen.

Find a full glossary of any tricky terms on page 70.

Time to test what you know. **Fill in the blanks below.** Don't be afraid to write in your book. Let's be joyful and create and play.

In the upcoming lessons, we're going to walk through how to create the letters you need to letter God's love using practice sheets. These will give you space to practice inside this book, but you can use your own paper for extra practice. **To photocopy extra practice sheets, turn to page 72.**

Lettering drills are structured in four parts.

1. An example of the shape or letter you're working on.

2. A grayed version with arrows showing you the direction to draw. The circles at the beginning of a line indicate a starting place. Pay close attention to the circles; some letters require you pick up your pen 2–3 times.

3. A grayed shape or letter to trace.

4. Space to freehand.

It looks like this:

Go ahead and practice.

Bonus tip: This is where tracing paper comes in handy. Lay a piece over each practice sheet for additional space. Don't worry—it's safe to use with brush-pens.

Brush Lettering Techniques

In brush lettering, letters are varied in weight or thickness. Downstrokes are thick while upstrokes are thin. This is a base skill of brush lettering.

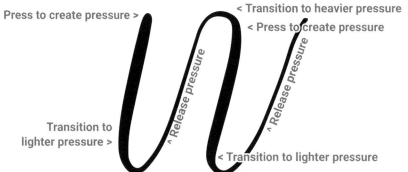

Each time you move in a down direction, you want to PRESS your brush more firmly onto the paper, creating a thick line by adding pressure on the tip. Each time you move in an upward direction, you will RELEASE the pressure, creating a thin line with the tip of your brush. The trickiness is in the transitions from thick to thin or vice versa.

Upstroke

Begin on the baseline. Make a soft and slow line with the tip of your brush at an angle up to cap height. The upstroke utilizes light pressure on your pen. Don't rush and make inconsistent dashes, but slow down and make each upstroke look uniform. Upstrokes tend to be a little wobbly, especially when you're using a new pen. Extra practice will give your hand the muscle memory you need to smooth out the upstroke.

Bonus tip: Lettering is muscle memory. Many of these drills may seem tedious or silly but are the foundations for beautiful lettering.

Lines

Starting at cap height, create thick, straight lines down to the baseline by adding pressure to your brush to test how thick you can get your ink. For the former tips, focus on using the side of your pen's tip to form a thicker line. *Bonus tip*: Avoid smooshing your pen into the paper or moving it in directions not instructed; this will ensure you don't fray your brush tip.

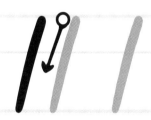

Downstroke

Start at cap height and taper into full pressure, then taper out at the baseline. The slower you go, the more you'll be able to notice the thickness and thinness transition. *Bonus tip*: Adding additional pressure to the flexible nib is what makes the thick stroke.

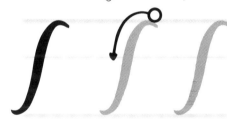

Overturn

Starting at the baseline, create a thin upstroke using the tip of your pen; transition into a thick downstroke at about 12 o'clock once you reach cap height (add pressure during the transition all the way to the bottom of the page). *Bonus tip*: Keep both the upstroke and downstroke parallel.

Underturn

Start at cap height with a thick downstroke (add extra pressure to increase thickness). At 6 o'clock, when you reach the baseline, transition into a lightly pressured upstroke using the tip of your pen. *Bonus tip:* Keep both the downstroke and upstroke parallel.

Compound Curve

Begin at the baseline with a light-pressured upstroke; at 12 o'clock, which is cap height, transition into the hard downstroke; at 6 o'clock, transition back into the thin upstroke. Take your time with the transitions. *Bonus tip:* Keep all three lines parallel.

Bonus Tip: If you are a lefty, see page 8 for extra coaching to master this transition.

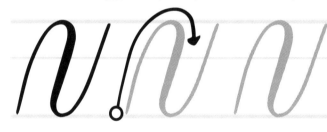

Oval

Begin at the 2 o'clock above the x-height with a thin upstroke that quickly transitions into a thick downstroke to the left, moving counterclockwise. At 6 o'clock, transition back into a thin upstroke to connect to the starting line.

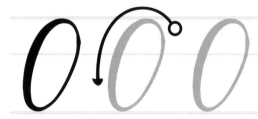

Ascending Loop

Begin at x-height with a light upstroke to cap height; transition at 12 o'clock into a thick downstroke all the way down to the baseline. *Bonus tip: Keep a consistent thickness and consistent thinness. The slower you write, the easier the consistency will be.*

Descending Loop

Begin at the x-height with a thick downstroke all the way to the beard line. At 6 o'clock, transition into a thin upstroke clockwise back toward the baseline, intersecting at the thick downstroke.

Ooh la la!

You're crushing it! Now that you've practiced your brushstrokes, let's transition to lowercase letters so you can start writing love letters to your friends and family.

Lowercase Letters

a *a a* a

B is for brave because that's what you are.

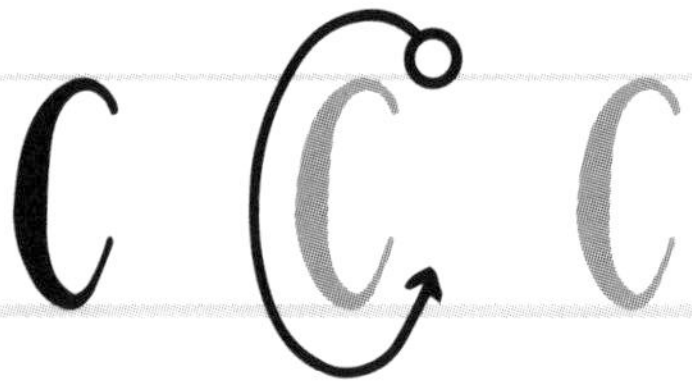

b *b b* b

Notice how the D combines the C plus an ascending loop.

c *c c* c

d *d d* d

Remember: The circles indicate when to pick up your pen.

e *e e* e

G is for we're glad you're here.

J is a descending loop, but don't forget the dot!

L is because you have the best laugh.

M requires three overturns (the letter, not Margaret).

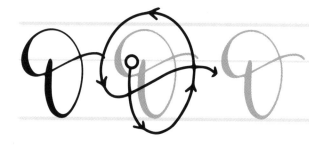

22

Ooh la la!

Use extra lines for more practice and play.

Uppercase Letters

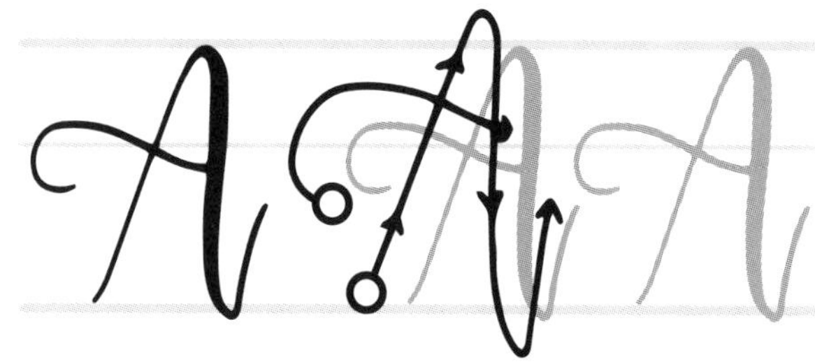

A A A

B combines an ascending loop with a lowercase Z.

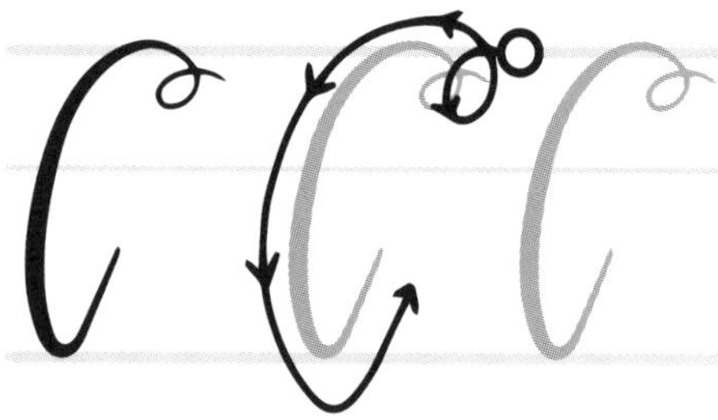

B B B B

C C C

D D D D

E is for enough because you are enough.

E E E E

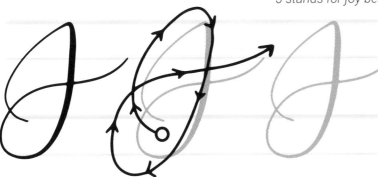

H combines a descending loop with a downstroke.

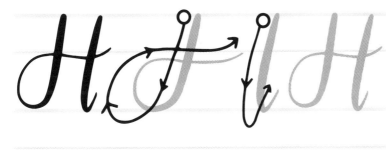

J stands for joy because you bring joy to everyone you meet.

K is for kindness because your presence is a balm.

M and N combine an ascending loop with overturns.

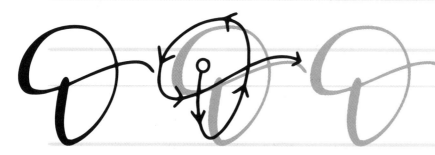

R requires you to pick up your pen three times.

T stands for thankful because we're thankful for you.

Well done!

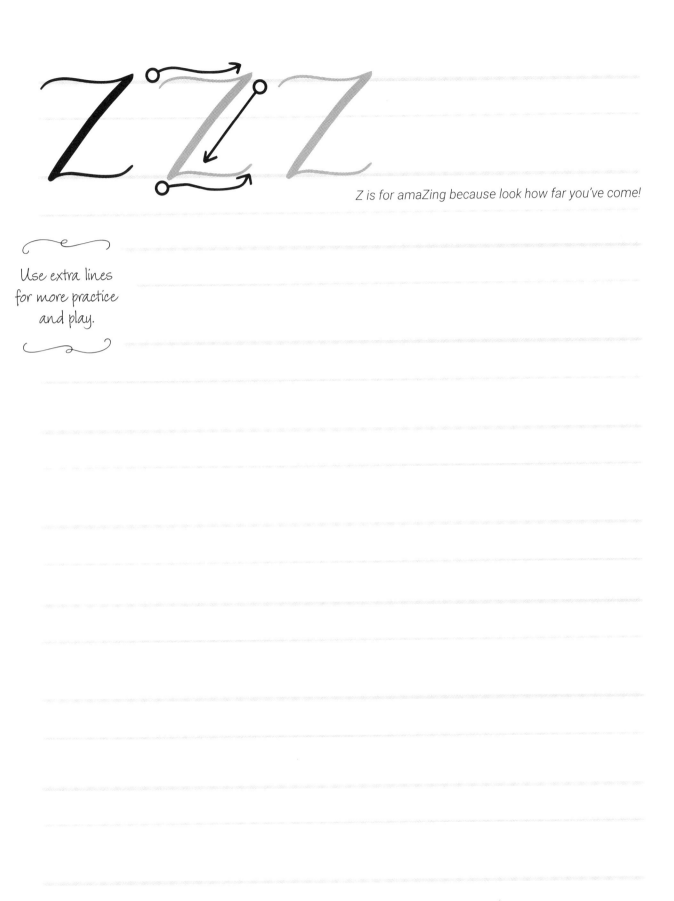

Z is for amaZing because look how far you've come!

Use extra lines for more practice and play.

Connecting Letters

You're doing so well. Now that you've crafted upper- and lowercase letters, let's learn to bind them together in love. Letters include a lead-in and/or an exit line. You practiced these on the previous pages. These lines are what are used to connect letters.

Let's practice connecting exit lines and lead-in lines. **Trace the word *joy*.** Notice the circled areas where the letters connect.

Remember to take it slow and lift your pen. When you learned cursive as a child, you were instructed to avoid picking up your pen between letters. Brush lettering asks you to slow down and handcraft each letter, picking up your pen between each letter form. On the word *Flourish* below, you'll find a circle each time the pen is lifted. Notice the pen lifts 12 times in this single word.

Practice writing the word *Flourish*. Lift your pen each time you form each letter.

Ensure readability. For example, a U connected to an R can look like a W. A lowercase F connected to an L can look like an uppercase H. That may alter the meaning a smidge. We discovered this when hand-lettering the cover of Margaret's devotional, *Flourish*. In the final design, we disconnected the U and R, as well as the F and L to ensure legibility.

All letters connected >

Select letters disconnected >

Final cover of *Flourish: A 52-Week Devotional with Coloring Pages* >

Write *Flourish* below. Lift your pen between letters and disconnect letters for added readability.

Keep your lines consistent in length and direction. Each lead-in and exit line in a word should be parallel. Place equal distance between each letter. Depending on your personal style, you can stretch letters long or keep them snug.

Write the word *snug* keeping your letters close together and short connections.

Write the word *long* stretching exit and lead-in lines and spacing your letters across.

For double letters (two of the same letter in a row), don't keep both letters identical. Adjust the height or size of the second letter so it looks unique. **Trace the double letters below.**

Struggling making the connections? Try disconnecting letters that begin with counterclockwise ovals (like lowercase A, C, D, G, and Q). Because you have to move farther down the page to start that letterform, smooth lead-in lines can be tricky. **Try below with the word *peace*.**

Lettering God's Name

Let's combine the lettering we've learned with growing closer to God. Below are two names of God found throughout Scripture and their meanings. As you letter each name, reflect on how you've discovered this aspect of God's character in your life.

Abba: *Father*. The intimate name for God as Father evokes warm affection and full confidence. (Mark 14:36; Romans 8:15)

El Shaddai: *God Almighty*. This refers to the God who nourishes, satisfies, and provides for God's people as a mother would her child. (Genesis 17:1; 35:11)

Letter your name below. In the extra space, write the meaning of your name.

Welcome to Bounce Lettering

Now that we've explored the basics, it's time to add your own unique style and flair—and even color outside of the lines. Bounce lettering is lettering that creates a bouncing illusion by exit lines dipping below the beard line and lead-in lines stretching above cap height.

Bounce lettering is what what makes your letters appear like they are bouncing across the page. You'll notice the cover of this book is done with bounce brush lettering.

It is important that you often return to the baseline to provide balance and centering to your word. Be sure to keep a consistent slant (the degree at which you're writing) and consistent line weights (thicknesses on downstrokes and upstrokes).

When writing out a word, play around with which exit lines should bounce. Let's try it together.

Notice how the base of the A, I, H, and U are still sitting on the baseline, but stretched the exit strokes of the A, T, H, U, and L below the beard line and the lead-in line of the F, H, and L above cap height. There's no right or wrong way to know which lead-in or exit lines to extend. Play around with what feels and looks right.

Now you give it a try. **Write the word *faithful*.** Stretch some of the exit lines of each letter below the beard line while keeping other letters sitting on the baseline.

Beautiful work! We can't wait to see your gorgeous letters on the page ahead.

Snap a picture of this page and post it on social media using #handletteringgodslove.

34

Flourishing

Flourishes are ornamental swoops and swirls added to letters to embellish designs. Flourishing takes practice and will add whimsy and beauty to your work.

Here are places to add flourishes:

- underneath a word or layout
- on the descender of letters like G, J, and Y
- on the swash of letters like A, F, and T
- on the ascender of letters like H, F, D, and L
- on the lead-in line of the first letter of a word
- on the exit line of the last letter of a word

Let's start with a simple flourish you can practice adding underneath a word or layout.
Trace them below. Use a similar pressure as you would for an upstroke.

Bonus tip: When flourishing, the downstroke and upstroke rules change. Keep all flourishes the same thin weight. The letters and words will contrast even more and be easier to read.

35

Here are examples of flourishes to add to ascenders and lead-in lines. **Practice below.**

H is for happy you're here.

We'll combine these letters on the next page to form truth and beauty.

Here are examples of flourishes to add to descenders and exit lines. **Practice below.**

G is for gorgeous work.

Let's practice basic flourishes together. **Trace the word *truth*, then write it yourself.** Notice how the lead-in line of the H is what crosses both Ts.

Great work! That is a simple and beautiful way to add a flourish to a word. Now let's go pro. Let's combine the more advanced flourishes. **Trace the word *beauty*.**

Your turn! **Write the word *beauty* using flourishes we've practiced.** Sketch it in pencil before using your brush-pen.

Words as Art

You have all the skills necessary to string together beautiful Scripture to hang around your house and gift to your friends. But first, let's talk composition.

Composition is the placement or arrangement of visual elements in a work of art. This technique is used in brush lettering when arranging letters and words on a page. Like composing a symphony or writing an essay, composition in brush lettering takes thought and organization.

Here's a 7-step process of composing a brush lettering piece of art using Scripture. You'll use these steps when hand lettering God's love on the devotional pages to come:

1. **Select a verse or portion of a verse.** Short is best—between 5 and 7 words is a good starting place. The fewer words to arrange, the easier to read. As you advance in your lettering skills, increase the word count. To walk you through this process, I chose:

   We love because he first loved us. —1 John 4:19

2. **Select the word or phrase (1 to 3 words) that you want to emphasize from step 1.** Read the passage several times over. Allow God's Word to pour over and into you. What pops off the page? What made you pause?

   After reading 1 John 4:19 several times, the word that stood out to me was *first*. A reminder that we don't earn God's love, but His love was freely given from the very start. This is the word I want to emphasize and noodle over while I create.

3. **Sketch this emphasized portion in a large script using pencil.** A pencil doesn't give the thick and thin lines like a brush-pen, but the erasability allows us to move words around. Grab a piece of scratch paper and practice with me. Here's a sketch:

4. **Stack the other words on top or below the emphasized portion.** Leave equal kerning (the space between letters) and equal line spacing (the space between lines of text). You want this to look like one uniform piece of art that has the same flow and feel. Think through what words or phrases sit best next to one another in your specific passage. Here's a sketch:

5. **Fill the gaps and empty space with these bonuses.** Sometimes the words are in order but it still doesn't look complete. Move letters up and down within a word. Increase the bounce lettering. Add flourishes.

Bonus tip: Count out the letters on each line to ensure they are lining up in the center of the page.

Here is the same art sketched with flourishes. You'll notice some of the letters are rough around the edges—that's totally normal when you're first sketching in pencil.

Notice the extra swash added to the opening W and crossbar of the T. The extra flourishes and swoops to the lead-in lines of the B. The tail of the R in "first" became the lead-in line for the D in "loved." These are just some ideas to bump up the beauty in your art.

6. **Sketch and erase as many times as necessary.** I sketch and erase many times before inking my design. By the end, my lap is covered in eraser crumbles. Don't be afraid to erase and start over if you're not happy with something. Remember: Each time you write the verse, you're embedding it deeper into your heart and mind.

7. **When you're happy with your composition, pull out your brush-pen.** Run a quick eraser over the pencil lines so only a faint outline remains. Then brush letter away! The final design is on the next page.

Bonus pro tip: If you're feeling wild, throw a different font into the mix. Make your emphasized phrase using serif letters or all capital letters instead of script. This will make it stand out even more.

We love because He first loved us.

1 John 4:19

Devotional Instructions

Look at how far you've come! From mastering basic strokes to learning your letters, from connecting letters to playing with advanced techniques like bounces and flourishes, you have grown so much. We're so proud of you, sweet friend.

And now for our favorite part:

Hand lettering God's love.

The slow intentionality of hand lettering provides a beautiful backdrop to memorize and meditate on God's Word.

On the following pages, you'll find 12 devotional entries with accompanying Scripture that will root you in God's steadfast love. Each passage is designed to be traced.

Then, on the page that follows, you'll have space to create your own masterpiece. You can doodle and dot, swirl and swoop. Add color and texture, patterns and pops.

Let's pray together before we begin.

Creator, cause your love to flow in us and through us
as we letter your Word. Amen.

We can't wait to see
what you create. Snap pictures
and share on social media using
#handletteringgodslove.

Let's letter!

Since you are precious and honored in my sight,
and because I love you,
I will give people in exchange for you,
nations in exchange for your life.

—Isaiah 43:4

I love you.

These three words rank among the most powerful you'll ever speak, you'll ever hear. They reverberate deep in your bones because those are words with which you are formed and fashioned, dreamed and destined. You are handcrafted in the love of God, by the love of God, for the love of God.

But sometimes you lose your way.

God knows this. That's why you've heard the refrain "I love you, I love you, I love you" as a sacred echo.

These words glow bright crimson as a beacon call for you to return home, folded into God's loving embrace. Abiding in this deep love is where you're fully alive, run wild and free, and discover who you're created to be.

Allow these words to wash over you today, refresh your soul, revitalize your spirit.

The following page is for practicing hand lettering God's love. Copy the composition above, or create your own. Use any version of Isaiah 43:4. Sketch your composition in pencil before inking on the page.

Since you are precious and honored in my sight,
and because I love you,
I will give people in exchange for you,
nations in exchange for your life.

—Isaiah 43:4

Whoever does not love does not know God,
because God is love.

—1 John 4:8

When was the last time you felt genuinely loved?

When it comes to pure love, God is the ultimate source.

"Beloved, let us love one another, for love is from God; and everyone who loves is born of God and knows God. The one who does not love does not know God, for God is love" (1 John 4:7–8 NASB).

Notice that John begins with "Beloved." With a single word, he embodies the message of loving one another. This affection is not based on our own works, but bestowed by the grace of God, because genuine love emanates from the character of God.

John reveals that deep love for one another doesn't begin within ourselves but originates in God. God is the only true source of love in the world.

As God's child, you are a beautiful display of the nature of God. John says this both in the positive and the negative. He says that those who know God love deep, but those who don't love deep don't know God.

You are invited to know God and His love more deeply. As you spelunk the depths, climb the heights, and explore the width of God's affection, you display the nature of God and learn to love God and others more.

Whoever does not love does not know God,
because God is love.

—1 John 4:8

Above all, love each other deeply,
because love covers over a multitude of sins.

—1 Peter 4:8

Have you ever attended a church gathering where everyone smiles and says they're "fine," yet beneath the surface, most of the people are anything but "fine"? Sometimes in the busyness of life, it's easy to water-ski on the surface of real issues. We cruise by each other, offer a wave, and keep going.

Time and time again throughout the Bible, we are urged to stop living at surface level and go deeper with those around us. We are challenged to find out how those in our community of faith are really doing.

God designed you for rich relationships, not shallow acquaintances.

But this doesn't happen without persistence and intentionality. Leverage everyday activities—the summer concert series, a backyard barbeque, an afternoon on the golf course or around the Ping-Pong table, a walk by the river—to ask deeper questions. "What are you reading?" "What are you learning at work that excites you?" and "If you could have one struggle in your life instantly vanish, what would it be?" can serve as gateway questions for deeper connection, relationships, and loving one another.

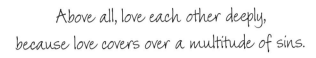

Above all, love each other deeply,
because love covers over a multitude of sins.

—1 Peter 4:8

The Lord's lovingkindnesses indeed never cease,
For His compassions never fail.

—Lamentations 3:22 NASB

I know in my head that God loves me, but all too often I don't sense divine affection in my heart.

Sometimes I feel like Dory in the animated movie *Finding Nemo*, or Lucy (played by Drew Barrymore) in *50 First Dates*. Wide-eyed and playful, I suffer from chronic spiritual short-term memory loss. As if each time God echoes love and compassion, it's just like the first time.

Perhaps God echoes love not because we're thickheaded as much as we're easily distracted. God repeats the message of love and compassion and mercies that never fail so we remain focused on what's most important, not just most imminent.

With each resounding echo of God's compassion, we rediscover that His mercies are new every morning and oh, how great is His faithfulness.

The Lord's lovingkindnesses indeed never cease,
For His compassions never fail.

—Lamentations 3:22 NASB

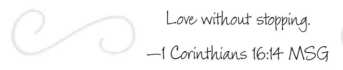

Love without stopping.

—1 Corinthians 16:14 MSG

Leif began singing a song over me soon after we were married. This was no ordinary song. The refrain lacked melody, harmony, rhyme. Perhaps it wasn't a song at all except to me.

After a spat or miscommunication, he'd wrap me in his arms and whisper in my ear, *"I'm never letting go. I love you. I picked you and I'm so grateful you picked me. Your saying 'yes' is the best thing that's ever happened to me."*

Without melody, this became the song Leif sang over me. He's been singing it ever since. I soon learned the chorus.

"I love my life with you. Thank you so much for picking me. There's no one I'd rather live this life with."

After almost 15 years of marriage, we don't wait for the hard or sad or mad or bad to whisper these words. We sing them in the morning with crispies in the corners of our eyes, and in the evening after a brutal day's work.

"Thank you for choosing me. There's no one I'd rather do this life with. Thank you for saying 'yes.' I'm the luckiest in the whole world."

My hope and prayer for you today is that you will sing a song of thanksgiving and blessing over those you love most. That you may remember to do everything in love, and remember that in everything you do you are loved.

Love without stopping.

—1 Corinthians 16:14 MSG

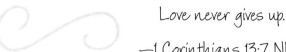
Tucked into the details of the arrival of Christ is the story of a stunning woman of faith. Luke 2:36–38 introduces us to Anna, who married young. She lived with her husband for seven years, then he died tragically, leaving her a widow.

She spent decade after decade of her life in the temple. While other women were supported by their spouse and children, Anna centered her life on God. She could have become bitter in her grief, but instead she established her life on gratitude and prayer. Scripture tells us that she prayed day and night.

At the age of eighty-four, she still refused to give up on God. She kept seeking, pursuing, and leaning into the depths of God's love. She refused to let go of the belief in the promised Messiah. One day, quite unexpected, she watched a young couple make an offering as they dedicated their child. But this was no ordinary child. This was the long awaited One, Jesus.

In God's unending love, rest assured that He never gives up on you and through His love, rest assured, you never have to give up on Him.

Love never gives up.

—1 Corinthians 13:7 NLT

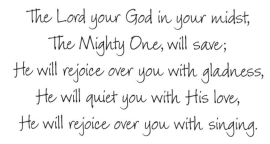

The Lord your God in your midst,
The Mighty One, will save;
He will rejoice over you with gladness,
He will quiet you with His love,
He will rejoice over you with singing.

—Zephaniah 3:17 NKJV

Zephaniah paints a picture of God as a victorious warrior who dances in wild delight over you with joy. He quiets you with his love and refreshes the recesses of your soul with divine affection. Yet in the everyday hustle of chores, errands, house maintenance, and work, we lose sight of this rich imagery. All our harried motion distracts us from the message of God's love.

As followers of Jesus, we know that God is with us, but how often do we take time to simply be with God and listen for His wild delight? How often do we allow God to refresh us with His love?

Much of our life is surrounded by noise until moments of silence vanish. If left un-checked, we can grow to fear silence, because without all those distractions, the thoughts and feelings we've been trying to avoid—worry, anxiety, doubt—float to the surface of our souls. Silence asks us to allow these emotions to emerge so that we can take them to God in prayer, asking for the comfort and guidance only God can give.

Through silence we accept the invitation to just be with God. To give time for God to echo love and for us to respond. To give space for prayer to lift from our lips. To lean into the renewal only God can give.

Today, pause in silence and ask God to refresh your life with love.

He will quiet you with his love.

The Lord your God in your midst,
The Mighty One, will save;
He will rejoice over you with gladness,
He will quiet you with His love,
He will rejoice over you with singing.

—Zephaniah 3:17 NKJV

I give you a new command: Love each other.
You must love each other as I have loved you.

—John 13:34 NCV

You are designed to be a conduit of God's love. Just as you freely receive God's love, you are to freely give God's love. Yet this love is more than kind thoughts and well-wishes; God's love manifests itself in action.

As followers of Christ, we're meant to use the gifts that God has given us for His glory and to demonstrate compassion to others. The spiritual practice of service demonstrates that we aren't only designed for relationship with God, we are designed for relationship with others, too.

When we walk in the way of Jesus, we bring freedom, healing, and justice to the world. Often that's expressed in meeting spiritual, relational, and physical needs. When you respond to opportunities to serve others, you not only serve Christ, you become more like him, too.

Engaging in loving service as a spiritual practice goes beyond when or how or who you serve, but also the attitude with which you serve. You can serve others for your gain—whether applause or appreciation—but Christ calls us to practice loving service when no one says thank you.

Consider the night of Jesus' arrest. All the disciples run away. One will become a traitor. Yet rather than throw in the towel, Jesus picks up the towel. He washes their feet.

Who do you need to love with abandon in your life? Who is Christ calling you to love just as He loved you?

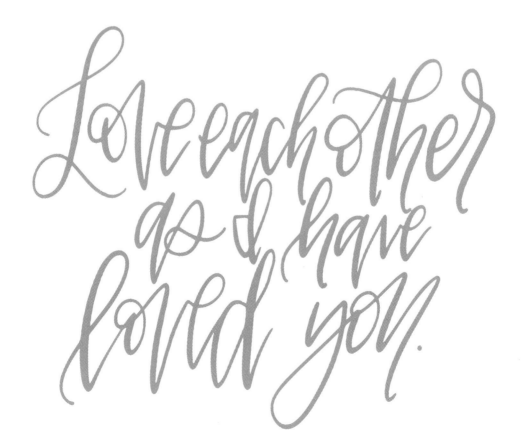

I give you a new command: Love each other.
You must love each other as I have loved you.

—John 13:34 NCV

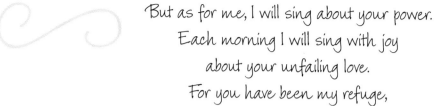

But as for me, I will sing about your power.
Each morning I will sing with joy
about your unfailing love.
For you have been my refuge,
a place of safety when I am in distress.

—Psalm 59:16 NLT

When was the last time you sang a favorite song at the top of your lungs? Or typed a passionate text to a friend? Or laughed so hard tears streamed down multiple places?

We have countless ways to express our joys and fears, our dreams and tears. And God leans in to hear every word and sound. But among the greatest expressions you'll ever make is thanks to God for His fierce love.

God is so extravagant in tender, patient care that He deserves gratitude and praise. You can offer your creative expression of love—through song or dance or even hand lettering.

Take time today to brush stroke an attribute of God, pen a sonnet of His love, or sketch a poem of divine affection. Remember that God delights in praise no matter what the shape or brushstroke through which your words of love appear.

In the morning I will sing of your LOVE.

But as for me, I will sing about your power.
Each morning I will sing with joy
about your unfailing love.
For you have been my refuge,
a place of safety when I am in distress.

—Psalm 59:16 NLT

Beloved, let us love one another,
for love is from God;
and everyone who loves is born of God
and knows God.

—1 John 4:7 NASB

I recently heard of a family with teenage children who committed to the practice of avoiding criticism on the Sabbath. The simple practice soon became a healthy habit for the family. They noticed more and more of the teenagers' friends coming over on Sunday just to hang out and be with the family.

None of them knew about the family's spiritual practice, but people were drawn to the life-giving conversation and fun.

Kind and encouraging words are a wondrous way to love one another. The way you speak can bring healing and bestow hope. You can instill courage and demonstrate compassion. You can fortify faith and present peace.

One of the most powerful ways that you can love someone today is through your words. Speak life into as many people as you can today.

Beloved, let us love one another,
for love is from God;
and everyone who loves is born of God
and knows God.

—1 John 4:7 NASB

*Because you are precious in My sight
and honored, and I love you,
I will give people in exchange for you
and nations instead of your life.*

—Isaiah 43:4 HCSB

God looks at you as His treasured child. You are invited to call on God anytime—24/7—knowing He leans close to listen to you. You can approach your heavenly Father with the confidence that He's got you and will never let go.

As a precious child of God, you receive an inheritance from Him. All the property of God, all the spiritual riches in Christ, both in this present life and in the life to come, are available to you. You are an heir. Each day, He showers an array of gifts on you—hope, strength, joy, peace, and many more—for you to enjoy and share with others.

Because God loves you fiercely, He doesn't leave you alone. He places you in family. Those who choose to follow Jesus are your brothers and sisters. Together, you are more powerful than alone. Not only do you strengthen one other, you showcase unity and love to the world.

God destined you for an abundant future. You are so valuable to God now and forever. This life is not the end of your story. This is just the beginning. You are destined for heaven. Jesus describes the Father's house as large and roomy. A breathtaking place is waiting for you.

The God of the universe sees you as so precious that He calls you His child, promises you an inheritance, places you in a holy family, and makes it possible for you to enjoy Him forever. Indeed, you are precious in God's sight.

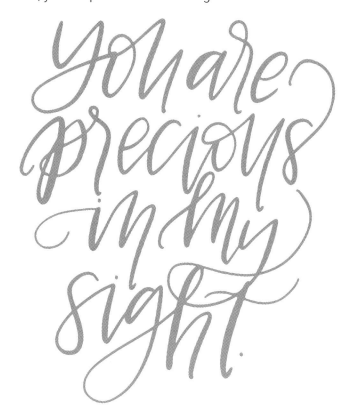

Because you are precious in My sight
and honored, and I love you,
I will give people in exchange for you
and nations instead of your life.

—Isaiah 43:4 HCSB

[Love] bears all things, believes all things,
hopes all things, endures all things.

—1 Corinthians 13:7 NKJV

One of the best descriptions of the love God has for you is found in 1 Corinthians 13. Often when this passage is read, especially at weddings, we think about its meaning in the way that we love others. But have you considered this is the way God loves you?

"[God's] love suffers long and is kind; [God's] love does not envy; [God's] love does not parade itself, [God's love] is not puffed up; [God's love] does not behave rudely, [God's love] does not seek its own, [God's love] is not provoked, [God's love] thinks no evil; [God's love] does not rejoice in iniquity, but rejoices in the truth; [God's love] bears all things, [God's love] believes all things, [God's love] hopes all things, [God's love] endures all things. [God's] love never fails." (1 Corinthians 13:4–8, "God's love" added for emphasis)

In everything, the love of God remains.

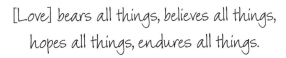

[Love] bears all things, believes all things,
hopes all things, endures all things.

—1 Corinthians 13:7 NKJV

sharing your work

Friend, we're so proud of how far you've come. Flip back to the very beginning and look at the progress you've made. It's time for a 10-second dance party! We're rejoicing with you.

Your beautiful art deserves to be shared and celebrated. From handmade birthday notes, dinner party invitations, framed art above the fireplace, and taped reminders on your bathroom mirror, it's time to wallpaper your house and life with God's love. Remember, you are fiercely loved by God.

Will you write down 3 names of people you want to encourage with God's love today? Make them a card, a note, or a frameable creation using hand lettering and one of the Scriptures we've worked through together.

1. _____

2. _____

3. _____

God's love isn't meant for us alone. We want it to splash off our fingertips everywhere we go.

You're amazing

Lettering Challenge

Your hand lettering journey doesn't stop here. Come along and hand letter God's love for the next 30 days. You'll be joining a community of friends from around the world.

1. Pray. Ask God to infuse you with His love.

2. Read the day's verse.

3. Reflect on the verse while you letter (refer to pages 39–42 for the layout process).

4. Snap a picture of your art and post it on social media using #handletteringgodslove. You never know whose life you may impact through that word of encouragement.

5. Click through the hashtag #handletteringgodslove and share love with your fellow letterers. Comment. Like. Share. Let's cheer each other on while we draw closer to God.

☐	Day 1	Exodus 15:13	☐	Day 16	1 John 3:1
☐	Day 2	1 Corinthians 13:1	☐	Day 17	Philippians 2:2
☐	Day 3	Proverbs 10:12	☐	Day 18	1 Corinthians 13:4
☐	Day 4	1 Peter 4:8	☐	Day 19	Psalm 86:15
☐	Day 5	John 14:15	☐	Day 20	1 Peter 3:8
☐	Day 6	1 Chronicles 16:34	☐	Day 21	Proverbs 8:17
☐	Day 7	Mark 10:21	☐	Day 22	Ephesians 4:32
☐	Day 8	Romans 12:9	☐	Day 23	1 Corinthians 13:8
☐	Day 9	Galatians 5:22	☐	Day 24	John 13:1
☐	Day 10	John 3:16	☐	Day 25	Psalm 36:5
☐	Day 11	1 Corinthians 16:14	☐	Day 26	1 John 4:9
☐	Day 12	Deuteronomy 7:9	☐	Day 27	Psalm 136:26
☐	Day 13	Proverbs 17:17	☐	Day 28	John 13:34
☐	Day 14	Colossians 3:14	☐	Day 29	Romans 12:10
☐	Day 15	Deuteronomy 6:6	☐	Day 30	1 Corinthians 13:13

Glossary

Ascender: The part of a letter that is taller than the x-height (like f or h). Often these extend beyond cap height.

Baseline: The line upon which most letters sit and below which descenders extend.

Beard line: This is where descenders end.

Bounce lettering: Lettering that creates a bouncing illusion by exit lines dipping below the beard line and lead-in lines stretching above cap height.

Brush lettering: Letters precisely drawn using a brush-pen with a flexible nib.

Cap height: The height of a capital letter above the baseline.

Composition: The placement or arrangement of visual elements in a work of art.

Descender: The part of a letter that extends below the baseline (like j or y).

Double letters: Two of the same letter in a row.

Downstroke: The thick, heavy-pressure stroke each time you move down.

Exit line: The exit stroke of a letter.

Flourish: An ornamental swoop and swirl added to and around letters to embellish designs.

Swashes: A flourish, such as an exaggerated serif, exit line, crossbar, or lead-in line.

Kerning: The adjustment of space between letters. Ideally, the space between brush letters should be equal.

Lead-in line: The entry stroke to a letter.

Nib: The tip of your brush or pen.

Overshoot: The distance a rounded lowercase letter (like a or o) exceeds the x-height.

Serif font: Typeface that has feet (serifs). Think Times New Roman.

Sans serif font: Typeface that doesn't have feet (serifs). The font you're reading is sans serif.

Upstroke: The thin, light-pressure stroke that forms each time you move up.

Weight: The thickness of your line on a downstroke or upstroke. This should be consistent throughout a word or phrase.

X-height: The distance between the baseline and the height of lowercase letters. This is measured by the height of the lowercase letter x in the font (hence the name).

Aa Bb Cc Dd

Ee Ff Gg Hh

Ii Jj Kk Ll

Mm Nn Oo

Pp Qq Rr Ss

Tt Uu Vv Ww

Xx Yy Zz

Meet Margaret

Margaret Feinberg (margaretfeinberg.com) is a popular Bible teacher and speaker at churches and leading conferences and creator of bestselling coloring books for grown-ups. Her books, including *The Organic God*, *The Sacred Echo*, *Scouting the Divine*, *Wonderstruck*, *Fight Back With Joy*, and their corresponding Bible studies, have sold over one million copies. Margaret lives in Utah with her husband, Leif, and their superpup, Hershey.

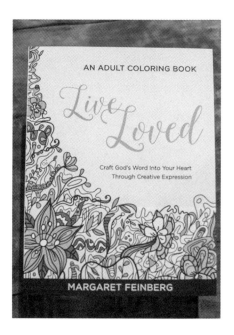

Visit margaretfeinberg.com to find
fresh Bible studies, When You Don't Know What to Say cards,
and Scripture-based coloring books.

meet Jessica

Jessica Richie (**jessicataylordesign.com**) combines her love for words and pretty things through hand lettering. She ushers people closer to Jesus through her Bible journaling and lettering classes. Jess and her fluffball pup, Elsa, live in Durham, North Carolina. Follow her adventures on Instagram: @jessicataylordesign.

Visit jessicataylordesign.com to find
your new favorite mugs, wall art, and thoughtful gift ideas.